Summary
of

Little Fires Everywhere
Celeste Ng

Conversation Starters

By BookHabits

Tips for Using BookHabits Conversation Starters:

EVERY GOOD BOOK CONTAINS A WORLD FAR DEEPER THAN the surface of its pages. The characters and their world come alive through the words on the pages, yet the characters and its world still live on. Questions herein are designed to bring us beneath the surface of the page and invite us into the world that lives on. These questions can be used to:

- Foster a deeper understanding of the book
- Promote an atmosphere of discussion for groups
- Assist in the study of the book, either individually or corporately
- Explore unseen realms of the book as never seen before

About Us:

THROUGH YEARS OF EXPERIENCE AND FIELD EXPERTISE, from newspaper featured book clubs to local library chapters, *BookHabits* can bring your book discussion to life. Host your book party as we discuss some of today's most widely read books.

Table of Contents

Introducing *Little Fires Everywhere* 5

Discussion Questions 9

Introducing the Author 30

Fireside Questions...33

Quiz Questions 44

Quiz Answers...57

Ways to Continue Your Reading...58

Introducing *Little Fires Everywhere*

L*ittle Fires Everywhere* takes place in a small town in Ohio called Shaker Heights. The main characters in the story are Bill and Elena Richardson, their children, Mia Warren, and her daughter, Pearl. The book is set in the late 1990s.

Elena Richardson, who is almost always called "Mrs. Richardson," is considered to be the perfect housewife of the 1990s. Her house, in a suburban area, is perfect as well, with its perfectly cut lawn. She tries to keep her household in perfect order, and she has also hired a housekeeper. Mrs. Richardson is a regular contributor to charities. She works as a reporter for a newspaper in Shaker Heights. Mrs. Richardson thrives on stability. She lives by her strict rules and instills these beliefs in her children, too. These rules are that a person must first attend college. Then, they should get married. After that, they should buy a house and have children. It was the birth of her daughter, Izzy, that caused her to have a need to control everything around her. Izzy had a traumatic birth and was born prematurely.

In the beginning of the book, there is a house fire. The house that starts on fire is owned by Bill and Elena Richardson. Bill and Elena have four children, who are all teenagers: Izzy, Moody, Trip, and Lexie. When the firefighters come to investigate the firefighters come to investigate the fire, they say that there were "little fires everywhere." There were many places that the fires were started. They found evidence that an accelerant was used, and they believe that the fires were started on purpose. The opinion of the town is that the suspect of the arson is a teenager, Izzy, who is known for being troubled and pulling pranks. However, Izzy is nowhere to be found. Mia Warren also disappeared along with her daughter Pearl, who is 15 years old. Mia and Pearl rented a small house from Bill and Elena.

The novel goes back in time to about a year earlier when Mia and Pearl first come to Shaker Heights. Mia and Pearl have traveled all around the United States in a VW Rabbit. They don't bring much with them, but one thing they do have is Mia's camera. They lived in numerous towns before they chose to settle down in Shaker Heights. Mia promises her daughter that they will stay in Shaker Heights. They rent a house from Bill and Elena, and Pearl often hangs around the Richardsons' house. The Richardsons and the Warrens are different people. The Richardsons are well-off, while the Warrens are less than wealthy. The Richardsons live settled, while the Warrens have lived a more nomadic lifestyle. Mia lives a more carefree lifestyle, and The Richardson's are structured. Elena sees Mia as a person who is breaking all of her rules and loosening the reins of control she has over her family and life.

In another part of town, there is a custody battle taking place. A Chinese-American child, who is one year old, has been raised by two American parents. Now, the baby's biological mother, Bebe, wants to take back custody of the baby. This divides the Richardsons and Warrens even more. The Richardsons take the side of the new parents. This couple have been close friends theirs for several years. They have wanted to have a baby for quite some time. On the other hand, Mia Warren shows support for Bebe. She understands that postpartum depression led Bebe to become desperate and abandon her child outside of a fire station.

Meanwhile, Elena has started to investigate Mia and her many secrets. Elena has started to see Elena as her enemy. Mia's daughter, Pearl, does not even know the details of Mia's past. When Pearl is asked where her mother grew up, Pearl replies that she is not sure, but thinks she may have grown up in California. Pearl is finally becoming close to people for the first time in her life – The Richardson children. She even finds herself in a love triangle between the Richardson sons. Unfortunately, Elena Richardson does not want Pearl's mother to be in her way any longer, which ultimately will hurt Pearl.

Little Fires Everywhere has been called "stunning" by *Booklist* and "intricate" and "captivating by *Publishers Weekly*. Author Terry McMillan praised Celeste Ng for her interesting characters, perfect details, and her honest writing. Finally, *Buzzfeed* wrote in their review that *Little Fires Everywhere* is a keen look into what it means to be a mother and what family, obsession, privelege, secrets, and perfectionism look like.

Discussion Questions

"Get Ready to Enter a New World"

Tip: Begin with questions dealing with broader issues to ensure ample time for quality discussions. Read through all discussion questions before engaging.

~~~

question 1

Little Fires Everywhere has many characters in it plot. Who was your favorite character, and why were they your favorite?

~~~

~~~

question 2

Mia Warren and Elena Richardson are different in many ways. In what ways are they similar?

~~~

~~~

question 3

The Warrens and The Richardsons are two families who appear in *Little Fires Everywhere*. How believable are they as characters and as families?

~~~

~~~

question 4

Elena Richardson sees Mia Warren as her enemy. Why do you think she sees
Mia in this way?

~~~

~~~

question 5

As the story goes on, Elena Richardson becomes more curious about the Warrens. She begins to ask more questions about their past. Why do you think she is motivated to investigate the Warrens?

~~~

~~~

question 6

Mia Warren and her daughter Pearl have moved around the United States many times. Mia tells Pearl that they will stay in Shaker Heights. Why do you think Mia chose Shaker Heights as the place to settle down?

~~~

~~~

question 7

One major source of conflict in the novel is the baby who was born to Bebe.
Bebe had post-partum depression and left the baby at a fire station. The baby
was adopted by new parents, but now, Bebe wants the baby back. Whose side
are you on in this conflict?

~~~

~~~

question 8

Consider the character of Pearl. How did Pearl change or grow throughout
the novel?

~~~

~~~

question 9

Mia Warren has lived a nomadic lifestyle for many years. What growth or change was there in Mia throughout the novel?

~~~

~~~

question 10

In *Little Fires Everywhere*, Izzy is known as the "problem child." Why was Izzy given this label? Why does everyone expect that she started the fire?

~~~

~~~

question 11

Elena Richardson likes to be in control and likes everything to have structure and order. Why do you think she lives her life in this way?

~~~

~~~

question 12

When word gets out that Bebe wants to take her baby back, Mia takes Bebe's side. Why do you think this is?

~~~

~~~

question 13

One passage from the book says that from time to time a person has to burn
everything and start over again. After the fire dies out the soil is able to grow
new things. The passage goes on to say that people are able to start again
after they "start fires." What are your thought on this passage?

~~~

~~~

question 14

Before it was revealed who started the fire, who did you believe started it?
Why did you suspect this person?

~~~

~~~

question 15

Think about when you found out who caused the fire. What was your
reaction to the reveal?

~~~

~~~

question 16

Little Fires Everywhere became a bestseller for *The New York Times* instantly after its release in 2017. Why do you think the book was so popular?

~~~

~~~

question 17

Author John Green stated that *Little Fires Everywhere* was his favorite novel of 2017. How does this novel stack up against others you have read this year?

~~~

~~~

question 18

Jodi Picoult, who is an author, said that she read *Little Fires Everywhere* in one sitting. What was your reading experience like?

~~~

~~~

question 19

According to Terry McMillan, the characters in *Little Fires Everywhere* are interesting. What were your overall thoughts on the characters in this novel?

~~~

~~~

question 20

In the opinion of one reader, Celeste Ng was able to change their perspective.
By the time they finished *Little Fires Everywhere*, their opinions drastically
changed from when they started reading it. How did your opinions change as
you read the story?

~~~

Introducing the Author

Celeste Ng is a native of Pittsburgh, Pennsylvania. Her parents are immigrants from China. They came to the United States in the later half of the 1960s. Her father had a job at NASA. He worked in the John H. Glenn Research Center as a physicist. Sadly, her father passed away in 2004. Ng's mother had a career as a chemist. She was a professor at Cleveland State University. Ng grew up with one sister. At the age of ten, Ng and her family moved away from Pittsburgh. They relocated to the city of Shaker Heights, Ohio. Ng went to school in Shaker Heights from elementary school through high school. At Shaker Heights High School, Ng became involved with a race relations student group. She was part of the group for three of her high school years. She also became involved with *Semanteme*, which was the school's newspaper. She eventually became the co-editor of *Semanteme*. In 1998, Ng completed her education and graduated from high school. As a child, Ng's favorite book to read was *Harriet the Spy*. As she got older, she became fond of *The God of Small Things* by Arundhati Roy.

Following her high school graduation, Ng went to Harvard University where she studied English. After graduating from Harvard, Ng went to the University of Michigan for graduate school. At the University of Michigan, Ng studied creative writing and earned a Master of Fine Arts Degree. She was the recipient of the Hopwood Award while attending the University of Michigan for a short story she wrote titled *What Passes Over*. While at the University of Michigan, Ng also worked as a writing teacher. She also taught writing at a non-profit writing center in Boston called GrubStreet.

In 2012, Ng released her story *Girls, At Play*. For this story, she was awarded the Pushcart Prize in 2012. She has published stories in literary magazines such as *Subtropics, One Story,* and *TriQuarterly*. She has also published essays in *The Millions* and *Kenyon Review Online*. Her first novel, *Everything I Never Told You: A Novel* was published in 2014 by Penguin Press. *Everything I Never Told You* is a thriller novel that takes place in Ohio during the 1970s. The novel was inspired by her own experiences with racism, as well as the experiences of her friends and family. In 2017, Ng published her second novel, *Little Fires Everywhere*.

Ng describes herself as a writer who is drawn to tragic stories. She is not good at adding humor into her stories. She enjoys studying how people act and react. She believes that writers often write about the things they are afraid of in order to manage or deal with them. For her, the thing that terrifies her the most is losing the people she loves. She does not know how she would go forward in life without them. From that fear, her stories grow.

Today, Ng lives in the Cambridge, Massachusetts area. She is married and has one child, a son, with her husband.

Fireside Questions

"What would you do?"

Tip: These questions can be a fun exercise as it spurs creativity among the readers by allowing alternate scene endings and "if this was you" questions.

~~~

question 21

Celeste Ng is a child of parents who immigrated to the United States from China. What unique experiences do you think Ng has had in the United States? How do you think these things inspire her writing?

~~~

~~~

question 22

Celeste Ng and her sister grew up in Shaker Heights, Ohio. Why do you think she chose Shaker Heights for the setting of her novel *Little Fires Everywhere*?

~~~

~~~

question 23

In her schooling year, Celeste Ng was the co-editor for her high school's newspaper. In what ways do you think this experience would help her in her later career as an author?

~~~

~~~

question 24

Celeste Ng has stated that it is difficult for her to write humorous stories, and it is easier for her to write stories that include tragedies. Why do you think this is?

~~~

~~~

question 25

Before becoming a fiction author, Celeste Ng began her writing career as an essayist and writer of short stories. Why do you think she made the switch to writing fiction novels?

~~~

~~~

question 26

Mia Warren believes that Bebe leaving her baby at the fire station was an act of desperation stemming from post-partum depression. How might the story be different if Bebe had not given away her baby?

~~~

~~~

question 27

Much of the conflict between the Richardsons and the Warrens seems to come from the Warrens living in the Richardsons' guest house. How would the story be different if Mia and Pearl Warren had chosen to live somewhere else? How would Pearl be affected if they did not live at the Richardsons?

~~~

~~~

question 28

Imagine you had the ability to be a character in the novel. Which character would you like to be and why?

~~~

~~~

question 29

Imagine you could sit down with the author and interview her. What
questions would you ask her?

~~~

~~~

question 30

Izzy's traumatic birth caused Elena to need control in many situations. What do you think Elena's personality would be if Izzy had not had a traumatic birth?

~~~

Quiz Questions

"Ready to Announce the Winners?"

Tip: Create a leaderboard and track scores to see who gets the most correct answers. Winners required. Prizes optional.

~~~

quiz question 1

Little Fires Everywhere takes place in _____,
Ohio. The main characters of the story are the Richardsons and the Warrens.

~~~

~~~

quiz question 2

Bill and Elena Richardson live in a suburban area with their _____
children. Mrs. Richardson is considered to be the perfect housewife.

~~~

~~~

quiz question 3

Mrs. Richardson lives her life by following a set of strict _____. She believes people should go to college, get married, then buy a house and have children.

~~~

~~~

quiz question 4

The book begins with a _____ in the Richardson house. According to
the town, the main suspect is Izzy.

~~~

~~~

quiz question 5

Mia Warren and her daughter, _____ move to Shaker Heights after living as nomads for several years. They rent the guest house from the Richardsons.

~~~

~~~

quiz question 6

True or False: Mia enjoys living a carefree lifestyle. This is in contrast to the Richardsons who live their life filled with structure and order.

~~~

~~~

quiz question 7

True or False: After Bebe leaves her child at the fire station, she realizes it was a mistake. She realizes that she was suffering from post-partum depression, and she wants her child back.

~~~

~~~

quiz question 8

Celeste Ng is the author of *Little Fires Everywhere*. She was born in
_____. She later moved to Shaker Heights,
Ohio with her family.

~~~

~~~

quiz question 9

The parents of Celeste Ng were immigrants from _____. Her
father worked at NASA as a physicist, and her mother was a chemistry
professor at Cleveland State University.

~~~

~~~

quiz question 10

Celeste Ng attended _____ University where she studied English. She later went to the University of Michigan where she studied creative writing for her Master's Degree.

~~~

~~~

quiz question 11

True or False: The first novel that Celeste Ng published was Little Fires Everywhere. The novel is about a young woman who runs away from home.

~~~

~~~

quiz question 12

True or False: Celeste Ng is currently living in Cambridge, Massachusetts.
She has one child with her spouse.

~~~

Quiz Answers

1. Shaker Heights
2. Four
3. Rules
4. Fire
5. Izzy
6. True
7. True
8. Pittsburgh, Pennsylvania
9. China
10. Harvard
11. False
12. True

Ways to Continue Your Reading

E VERY month, our team runs through a wide selection of books to pick the best titles for readers and reading groups, and promotes these titles to our thousands of readers – sometimes with free downloads, sale dates, and additional brochures.

Want to register yourself or a book group? It's free and takes 1-click.

Register here.

On the Next Page…

Please write us your reviews! Any length would be fine but we'd appreciate hearing you more! We'd be SO grateful.

Till next time,

BookHabits

"Loving Books is Actually a Habit"

Made in the USA
Middletown, DE
03 November 2017